Christmas Long Ago

Marian I. Doyle

MADE IN ENGLAND

Christmas Greetings..

Merry Christmas

Joyful Christmas Greetings.

Schiffer Publishing Ltd

4880 Lower Valley Road, Atglen, PA 19310 USA

Other Schiffer Books by Marian I. Doyle
An Illustrated History of Hairstyles: 1830-1930

Other Schiffer Books on Related Subjects
Christmas Through the Decades, by Robert Brenner
*Christmas 1940-1959: A Collector's Guide to Decorations
    and Customs*, by Robert Brenner
*Christmas 1960 to the Present: A Collector's Guide to
    Decorations and Customs,* by Robert Brenner
*Christmas Plates: from Royal Copenhagen and Bing &
    Grondahl,* by Lars Christofferson
One Hundred Years of Valentines, by Katherine Kreider
Thanksgiving and Turkey Collectibles: Then and Now, by
    John Wesley Thomas & Sandra Lynn Thomas

Copyright © 2006 by Marian I. Doyle
Library of Congress Control Number: 2006928948

Designed by John P. Cheek
Cover design by Bruce Waters
Type set in Seagull Hv BT/Caslon 224 Bk BT

ISBN: 0-7643-2357-1
Printed in China

394.2663
DOY

Published by Schiffer Publishing Ltd.
4880 Lower Valley Road
Atglen, PA 19310
Phone: (610) 593-1777; Fax: (610) 593-2002
E-mail: Info@schifferbooks.com

For the largest selection of fine reference books on this and related subjects, please visit our web site at www.schifferbooks.com
We are always looking for people to write books on new and related subjects. If you have an idea for a book please contact us at the above address.

This book may be purchased from the publisher.
Include $3.95 for shipping.
Please try your bookstore first.
You may write for a free catalog.

In Europe, Schiffer books are distributed by
Bushwood Books
6 Marksbury Ave.
Kew Gardens
Surrey TW9 4JF England
Phone: 44 (0) 20 8392-8585;
Fax: 44 (0) 20 8392-9876
E-mail: info@bushwoodbooks.co.uk
Website: www.bushwoodbooks.co.uk
Free postage in the U.K., Europe; air mail at cost.

Contents

Introduction

We haven't always known how to feel about Christmas. Even in England, where it had traditionally been a riotous twelve-day celebration, there came an extensive period of disapproval to taint the festivities—the same period that brought the Puritans to America in the early 1600s. They arrived in New England with a distaste for Christmas and its excesses that suppressed celebration there for over a century. The settlers of Jamestown, Virginia, had made the trip earlier, however, and were largely free of Puritanical prejudices. For them, Christmas was a holiday from the first, while the Dutch of New Amsterdam, like many of their European relatives, ignored the dour Puritans altogether to make the time a joyful feast.

"What differences have there not been about Christmas, the grand anniversary of christendom; have not some been for the celebration and observation of it and some not, have not some called it a holy-day and some with propriety a folly day," wrote Dr. Alexander Hamilton from Maryland in 1746. America's Yuletide complexities were interesting enough to be reported in an 1818 edition of *Nile's Register*. Boston, it was noted, somewhat observed the holiday by closing businesses and holding evening concerts of sacred music. New York's theaters remained open on Christmas, while in Philadelphia perhaps half the people "paid some attention" to the occasion.

By the Victorian era, the dispute had happily been resolved. Christmas made a glorious return, bringing with it many of the old customs and beliefs. If the celebration was a bit less lusty, it was far more kindly, defined for all time by Charles Dickens in his 1843 story, "A Christmas Carol." Queen Victoria and her German husband made the Christmas tree fashionable, Clement Moore told us what Santa Claus looked like, and Thomas Nast gave the description artistic substance. Even New England shook off its Puritanical scruples to become America's idyllic image of Christmas as it ought to be.

"The kindly season of gifts and compliments has come round again," *Harper's Monthly* said in December of 1854. "Lights are put in the windows, and hearts are lighter and eyes brighter. There is loud laughter of children in the early morning as they peep into and feel of the stocking hanging by the chimney. There is quieter pleasure later around the ample table, heaped with presents, and a fairy gayety at evening about the sparkling Christmas-tree."

Chronologically, the Victorian era ended with the death of its queen in 1901. Ideologically, however, it lasted until shattered by the stark realities of World War I. Yet when it comes to Christmas, we are all still Victorian. We embrace their version of the celebration both merry and moral, and we yearn for a holiday more like theirs. Christmas was the Victorians' gift to us. This book is meant as a gift to all who hold Christmas in their hearts, regardless of the date.

Chapter One
Chill December

And after him came next the chill December:
Yet he, through merry feasting which he made
And great bonfires, did not the cold remember;
His Saviour's birth his mind so much did glad.

—From Spenser's "The Faerie Queen"

No better time could be found for a celebration than in the bleakest of seasons when needed most. There is something about it that heightens the festivity, according to Washington Irving: "The dreariness and desolation of the landscape, the short and gloomy days and darksome nights… make us more keenly disposed for the pleasure of the social circle." Winter was, according to the 1857 editor of *Harper's Monthly*, the "enjoyable season of household life" when families, free of the exertions of summer, gathered at the hearth to share roasted chestnuts and apples. They drank mulled cider and retold old stories, and in the flickering flames their Christmas dreams were born.

'Twas Christmas-tide. With tales and talk
That never seemed to tire,
The children, gay with holiday
Sat round the blazing fire.

—From "The Happiest Christmas,"
by Margaret J. Preston, c.1885

Old Winter, cold winter again is here,
With his snow, his ice and rain,
The choicest old fellow of all the year,
We welcome him back again.

—From "Winter," by George Johnson, 1850

7

Christmas Greetings

If the morning drives are extended beyond the city, there is much to delight the eye. The trees are cased in ice; and when the sun shines out suddenly, the whole scene looks like one diffused rainbow, dressed in a brilliancy which can hardly be conceived of in England.
—Harriet Martineau, c.1835

As pleasant as the fireside was, the urge to be out and about was irresistible. In the country, men made excuses to go to the general store or post office and linger around the comfortably hot stove with other winter fugitives. In cities and towns, people organized scenic excursions into the country.

To venture outside was to be prepared. Heavy lap robes of felt, wool, and hide were piled into carriages and sleighs. Foot warmers were welcome companions, some filled with hot coals, some holding a heated slab of soapstone. Every home owned a bootjack to pry soaked leather boots off frigid feet. Long underwear, introduced to the country by the Union army during the Civil War, was worn in red flannel by men and in fine, soft wool by women and children. Felt, flannel, and wool were the most practical fabrics of the season, yet fashion sometimes trumped practicality. After all, there would soon be holiday parties and dances to attend, and every girl longed to look her best. The journal of one Victorian woman spoke clearly of this eternal feminine passion:

> I wonder if my descendants, should they ever read these memoirs, will be shocked at the levity of an ancestress who frankly acknowledged that the most vivid recollection left in her mind is a grey merino pelisse and black beaver hat and plumes, with which her small person was decked during the winter of 1859.

A Happy Christmas

A Merry Christmas

'Twas Christmas morn! Lo, on the Square
Snow-draped in wintry dress,
I met two buds of Vanity Fair
Whom wealth and fortune dress.

—From "Good Cheer," by Charles
Edward Barns

Christmas
Greetings

MY FIRST MUFF.
BY F. C.

HERE'S my little lady,
 Dressed with thoughtful care,
Smiling at the sunlight,
 Smiling at the air.

Whither, little lady,
 Whither shall we go?
O'er the lofty hill-tops—
 Through the winter's snow?

Will you with me wander
 Through the copses bare,
Where the dead leaves linger?—
 Autumn left them there.

No, my little lady;
 Snows would damp your feet;
Thorns would tear your jacket,
 Trimmed with ermine neat.

I will fetch a carriage,
 Drawn by ponies fine,
Lined with silken cushions,
 Fit for lady mine.

We will drive right swiftly
 O'er the hill-tops then—
Drive as quick as lightning
 Through the merry glen.

Then my little lady
 Safe from harm will be,
And her rich soft ermine
 From sharp thorns be free.

USE
CHADWICK'S SPOOL COTTON.

Little Miss Bessie
　　Has a new muff,
And fur gloves to keep her
　　Hands warm enough.
Mamma will let her
　　Run in the snow,
No matter how keenly
　　The wind may blow.

A Merry Christmas

Winter and youth seemed made for each other. As Christmas approached, get-togethers increased. Frolics in the snow, coasting parties, skating, and sleighing each heightened the anticipation, as holiday spirit was nurtured in December's snow.

CHRISTMAS GREETINGS

A Merry Christmas

Making a snow statue forms a capital amusement when the fields 'put on their winter's robe of purest white,' and the icicles hang glistening from the eaves...the statue should be rounded and shaped as neatly as possible; and, if the young artists possess ingenuity enough to make their work look something like a man, and not a heap of snow, so much the better. The modelers now, by common consent, withdraw to a stated distance and begin to pelt their handy-work with snow-balls, until the gigantic figure falls, feature by feature, amidst the shouts of the joyous throng.

—*The Boy's Treasury Of Sports, Pastimes, And Recreations*, 1854

Merry Christmas.
May all that life
can hold of joy,
be yours this happy day.

A Merry Christmas

A Merry Christmas to you

R. Ford Harper

HOLIDAY COMPLIMENTS of JOSEPH HORNE & CO.'S

"PLEASE SIR IT WASN'T ME"

A MERRY CHRISTMAS & A HAPPY NEW YEAR

Retail Stores, 197, 199 & 201 Penn Avenue, Pittsburg, Pa.

The skaters are out on the ice-bound stream,
Whirling around and about—
Hark! Hark! With overfraught joy they scream
And laugh, and hello and shout.

—From "Winter," by George Johnson, 1850

A Joyful Christmas

A Merry Christmas and A Ha...

Peerless Ink Cream
Saves Time and Money

It is the FASTEST SELLER on the Market

(OVER)

T73

USE
ACME SOAP.
(CUT FULL POUNDS.)

BEST BAR SOAP
MADE.

USE
LUTTED'S
COUGH DROPS

TOBOGGANING

Christmas
Remembrance

Christmas
Greetings

21

You may see boys coasting on Boston Common all the winter day through; and too many in the streets where it is not so safe. To coast is to ride on a board down a frozen slope; and many children do this in the steep streets which lead down to the Common, as well as on the snowy slopes within the enclosure where no carriages go. Some sit on their heels on the board, some on their crossed legs. Some strike their legs out, put their arms a-kimbo, and so assume an air of defiance amid their velocity. Others prefer lying on their stomachs, and so going head foremost; an attitude whose comfort I never could enter into.
—Harriet Martineau, c.1835.

Merry Christmas
and
Happy New Year
from
Uncle Theo   Dennison's CHRISTMAS POST CARD.

Merry Christmas

WJW

X-MAS GREETINGS

Snow! Snow! velvet snow,
    Everywhere you see;
Earth is like a frosted pound-cake,
    So it seems to me!

—From "A Merry Christmas" by George
        Cooper, date unknown

JOHN L. MOORHOUSE,
➤❋ DRY GOODS ❋◄
NO. 35 FIFTH AVENUE,
Pittsburgh, Pa.

When winter came, the maiden's heart
Began to beat and flutter;
Each beau would take his sweetheart out
Sleigh-riding in a cutter.

—**Harper's Monthly, 1854**

> *Swift as the lithe and eager hound,*
> *Away the merry sleighers bound!*
> *With jingling sound of bells they go;*
> *With hoofs that hardly touch the snow.*
>
> **—From "The Sleighers," by N. G. Shepherd, 1861**

How the hard-pressed snow squeaked beneath the gliding runners as with prancing span and jingling bells you sped down through the village street, with waving handkerchiefs and cheerful greetings right and left...Now you speed through a mist of drifting snow and the rosy cheeks tingle with the stinging icy flakes flying before the wind.

—Wm. Hamilton Gibson, 1880.

A MERRIE XMAS

Let me be merry now, 'tis time,
    The season is at hand
For Christmas rhyme and Christmas chime;
    Close up, and form the band.

**—From "Christmas Comes Again" by Elizabeth
Stoddard in *Appleton's Journal*, 1870**

Chapter Two
Deck The Halls

Bring me a garland of Holly,
  Rosemary, Ivy and Bays;
Gravity's nothing but folly
  Till after the Holidays.

—Harper's Monthly, January 1866

Bringing in the greens was one of the happiest outdoor events of the holidays, at least for those living in the country. Some made it an outing for the young, some made it a family tradition, still others made it a seasonal business, driving wagons heaped with evergreens of every sort to city markets where they were eagerly bought. Pine boughs, ivy, and holly adorned homes and churches along with ground pine, laurel, and the colorful accent of bittersweet berries. Mistletoe, tainted by its Druid past, was purchased to tickle the amorous fancy.

The evergreens were thrown down in the hall, and a hundred hands were soon busy making wreaths. On the ensuing evening, when the toil was over, some magical hand seemed to have decked the hall. Everywhere wreaths, festoons, zigzags, garlands—on the walls, the ceiling—above the pictures, the windows, and the doors—there was not a single spot where evergreens could go, which the hands of the young girls and their assistants had not decorated. It was a forest palace...
—"Our Christmas At The Pines," *Harper's Monthly*, 1857

A Happy Christmas

Merry XMAS

Merry Christmas

Out of the snow,
With pine and with holly
We'll trim up the house
And won't we be jolly!

Spread out the laurel and the bay,
For chimney-piece and window gay;
Scour the brass gear—a shining row,
And Holly place with Mistletoe.

—From "The Mistletoe" by Hone in
Harper's Monthly, 1866

A Merry Christmas AND a Happy New Year

A Merry Christmas

To wish you ALL HAPPINESS FOR THE CHRISTMASTIDE.

33

> Lo! In the woods, beneath the frost-kissed hill,
> The holly lights the path—December's rose—
> And underneath the scarlet berry grows,
> As if to tell us Love is living still.
>
> —From "A Christmas Thought" in *Harper's Monthly*, 1882

The Youth's Companion of 1900 suggested wiring bright red berries, raisins, red and green gumdrops, and colorful fine ribbons to a fresh green bough of holly. After topping the bough with some golden wheat or perhaps a large bow, it was to be presented to a friend or neighbor along with the following rhyme:

If the raisins keep soft and the berries bright,
On the bough of plenty, till the seventh night,
Your heart will be happy, your burden light
And your home filled with plenty.
Says the holly, if green,
"Good luck you will have until Christmas comes again
With sunshine all between."

—From "Getting Ready For Christmas," *The Youth's*
Companion, 1900

A Merry Christmas

A BRIGHT HAPPY CH

A HAPPY CHRISTMAS.

Let sinned against and sinning
Forget their strife's beginning,
    And join in friendship now:
Be links no longer broken,
Be sweet forgiveness spoken,
    Under the holly bow.

—**Charles MacKay**

Best Wishes FOR A Merry Christmas

A MERRY CHRISTMAS

Merry Christmas

May Fortune
smile upon thy path
And give thee of the best
she hath.

In 1829, the poinsettia was introduced by and named for Joel R. Poinsett, United States Ambassador to Mexico. Tristram P. Coffin, in his 1973 book of Christmas folklore, recounted the legend of a peasant boy who prayed one Christmas Eve for something worthy to place on the altar in honor of Christ's birth. When he stood, exquisite red petals sprang from the earth on which he'd knelt, and these he carried into the church.

Even Coffin doubted the age and authenticity of this story, however, and very little was written about the poinsettia's history by the Victorians. Nonetheless, they were enchanted with the plant and its flaming petals that so resembled the star of Bethlehem as it must once have blazed in the same season. While not an evergreen, the poinsettia bloomed at the time of the Christmas festival and it quickly achieved equal status in the affections of Americans.

MERRY CHRISTMAS

Christmas greetings.

Christmas greetings.

SINCEREST WISH
THAT NOTHING
HAPPINESS
THIS CHRISTMAS

WISHING YOU A
MERRY CHRISTMAS
AND THAT ITS MEM
ORY WILL LAST FOREVER

FRIENDSHIP'S CHRISTMAS WISH.

Make new Friends, also
But keep the old:
The first are silver,
The second, gold.

May yours be treasures
And wealth untold
In precious Friendships
Both new and old.

Christmas Greetings

38

A number of legends exist to explain the origin of the Christmas tree. One involves St. Winfrid, who was known for his conversions of Druids to Christianity. In front of a gathering of converts one night he began chopping at an oak—the most sacred Druid tree. As he labored to bring it down a sudden gale swept through the forest, shattering the oak into four sections. Where it had stood, a young fir now pointed toward the stars.

"This little tree, a young child of the forest, shall be your holy tree tonight," Winfrid told the people. "It is the wood of peace, for your houses are built of the fir. It is the sign of an endless life, for its leaves are ever green. See how it points upward to heaven. Let this be called the tree of the Christchild; gather about it, not in the wild wood, but in your own homes; there it will shelter no deeds of blood, but loving gifts and rites of kindness."

We greet you the time is here
When memory gathers up
The scattered links of friendship
And all is one dear Christmas cheer.

Dr. C. McLanes' Liver Pills —CURE— Malarial Diseases.

Xmas

Christmas Greetings!

December
25

A
Merry
Christmas

Another widely told legend—and the most accepted—gives credit for the Christmas tree to Martin Luther. While traveling in the snowy mountains one Christmas Eve, the story goes, Luther was struck by the brilliant beauty of the stars as they winked and sparkled through the branches of the trees. When he arrived home, he tried to describe the scene to his wife and children. Suddenly he rushed outside to return with a small fir. Fastening candles to its branches as a visible demonstration, Luther began the tradition of the Christmas tree.

Though the custom of the Christmas tree swept much of Europe, it only reached full popularity in Great Britain after being introduced by Queen Victoria, who had wholeheartedly adopted the delightful custom from her husband's homeland. Visiting America in 1835, Harriet Martineau saw the very first Christmas tree to be set up in the country village of Hingham, near Massachusetts Bay. It was in the home of a pastor, where a multitude of family and friends had gathered. In the midst of the games and laughter they were called into a side room to see a surprise—a Christmas tree hung with sweet treats and alight with candles.

"The children poured in," Miss Martineau wrote, "but in a moment every voice was hushed. Their faces were upturned to the blaze, all eyes wide open, all lips parted, all steps arrested." When the tree and its fruits had been enjoyed and the evening was over, the children went home to dream of the wonderful tree and to tell others of what they had seen.

Christmas trees were ornamented with a mix of homemade and store-bought trimmings. Walnut shells and pinecones were gilded, cone-shaped cornucopias were filled with candies, brilliantly colored die-cut scrap decorations were pasted onto gilt and lace papers or suspended by ribbons alone from branches alongside holiday postcards and sparkling glass balls. Paper chains and popcorn strings festooned the limbs where fruit and sweets waited to be found by tiny fingers. Best of all, small gifts nestled among the green needles—dolls, toys, and other wonderful things to be handed down to eager hands on Christmas Eve or Christmas Day in homes and churches.

This beautiful custom, which we have taken from the Germans, has struck such deep roots in our homes that, even, the poorest family will deny itself both food and clothing so as to obtain the wherewithal to purchase a little tree, and trim it with little trifles that will give great joy to the childish heart.
—From "The Fashion," by Georgiana Hull, in *Good Housekeeping*, 1885

I've hung a happy Wish or two, upon the Christmas Tree for You.

A Merry Xmas

A Merry Christmas

Christmas Greetings

In 1884, the New Orleans Exposition created a Christmas celebration for children. In the Great Hall, brilliantly lit by Edison electric lights, stood a perfectly shaped hemlock forty-five feet high, loaded with gifts. "What lovely gifts they were!" *Harper's Young People* reported. "Nothing that a child could want was missing—dolls, chairs, wardrobes, watches, clocks, tables, jumping-jacks, woolly dogs, sheep, birds, cages, sugar-plums, fiddles, drums, work-boxes, trinkets—everything to delight the thousands of happy children that waited expectantly around the tree…"

The gifts were distributed by Santa Claus as played by one of the Exposition commissioners dressed in a Siberian seal and reindeer skin outfit worn during two Arctic expeditions. The elaborate celebration stood as proof of the Victorian love for Christmas, children, and the Christmas tree.

There's a dear old tree,
And it blossoms once a year.
'Tis loaded with fruit from top to root,
And it brings to all good cheer.

For its blossoms bright are candles white
And its fruit is dolls and toys.
And they all are free for both you and me
If we're good little girls and boys.

—From "The Dear Old Tree" by Luella Wilson
Smith, 1907

The damsel donned her kirtle sheen;
The hall was dressed with holly green;
Forth to the wood did merry men go
To gather in the mistletoe.

—From "Marmion" by Sir Walter Scott

A MERRY CHRISTMAS

COPYRIGHTED 1908 BY JULIUS BIEN & CO. N.Y.

Wishing you a Merry Christmas

A plant sacred to the Druids, mistletoe came down to the Victorians trailing superstitions. Placed on the bedroom doorsill it would prevent nightmare. Sprigs preserved through the year served as a remedy for epilepsy and convolutions. Mistletoe's most intriguing powers, however, were romantic.

Three mistletoe leaves, each named for prospective lovers, were placed on hot coals. The first to pop was the one who loved best. And of course there was the "swift, sweet, coy game" beneath the hanging sprig where the victor picked a berry to commemorate the kiss and kept it for luck, while the hapless girl who received nothing beneath the mistletoe but despair was doomed to remain single for the year.

Many a maiden's cheek is red
By lips and laughter thither led;
And flutt'ring bosoms come and go
Under the Druid mistletoe.

—From "The Mistletoe" by Hone, 1865

In 1855, the editor of *Harper's Monthly* wondered why our Puritan ancestors disapproved so strongly of Christmas traditions such as mistletoe. "Is it, perhaps, heathenish?" he asked. "Heathenish? Just try it and see if it be heathenish. Yes, let even the Reverend Cotton Mather try it, and see if he does not like it, so that, upon coming out from the shade of the mistletoe, the Reverend Doctor Cotton Mather shall sing as the Reverend Martin Luther sang:

Who loves not wine, woman and song,
He is a fool his whole life long.

—From "Editor's Easy Chair," *Harper's Monthly*, 1855

YOU WILL BE WELCOME HERE THIS XMAS.

Isn't it strange that girls will go
And stand beneath the Mistle
And when they're kissed will loudly
They didn't know the Mistletoe was

MERRY CHRISTMAS

"Fortunately, the old, old fashion of the evergreens becomes newer every year," wrote *Scribner's Monthly* in 1870. Boughs, branches, sprigs and sprays of green made the Victorian home fragrant with a forest spice that created the perfect setting for Christmas wishes and Yuletide kisses and dreams enough to last the holiday through.

Chapter Three
The Spirit of Gifting

Tie up your parcels with ribbons gay;
Sprig them with green in the good old way.

—From "The Sign Of The Christmas Tree"
by Pauline Francis Clamp

A Merry Christmas

A Merry Christmas

A Merry Christmas

A Merry Christmas

"The chief delight of Christmas is the happiness of the children—the next is the Christmas shopping," *Harper's Monthly* said in 1868. For Victorians, gift buying was as frenzied during Christmas week as it is for us. "Every shop is crowded with busy buyers," *Scribner's Monthly* reported in 1871. "Papas and mammas laugh in each others faces as they stand side by side, squeaking the dolls and enumerating the dishes of the toy dinner-set. Little people with little pockets flatten anxious noses against great shop windows, intent upon stretching a small sum over many large relatives. Grandmammas, whose white cap-strings have many times of late been pushed aside to make room for whispering lips, go about, list in hand, determined that each child shall have its wish."

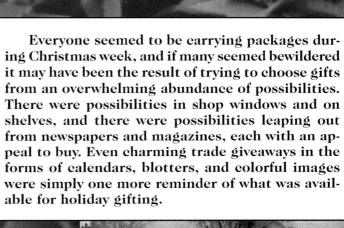

A LOAD OF GOOD WISHES FOR A MERRY CHRISTMAS

Everyone seemed to be carrying packages during Christmas week, and if many seemed bewildered it may have been the result of trying to choose gifts from an overwhelming abundance of possibilities. There were possibilities in shop windows and on shelves, and there were possibilities leaping out from newspapers and magazines, each with an appeal to buy. Even charming trade giveaways in the forms of calendars, blotters, and colorful images were simply one more reminder of what was available for holiday gifting.

A Joyful Christmas to You!

GREETINGS

Christmas Greetings

TAKE ADVICE FROM
SANTA CLAUS
AND GET A GOOD
SUPPLY OF

LUNDBORG'S CHOICE PERFUMES

LU...
P...

VICTOR
Bicycles
Make
The
Pace

Merry Christmas To All.
& A HAPPY NEW YEAR

A. G. SPALDING & BROS.
SPECIAL AGENTS.
NEW YORK. PHILADELPHIA.

A NEW STYLE
BISSELL CARPET SWEEPER
IS THE QUEEN OF
Christmas Presents.

It will make a pleasure of labor, lighten drudgery, save dust and
wear and back-aches. They are beautiful machines, and lasting,
perfect sweepers—our modern styles.

LOOK FOR THE WORD BISSELL'S
—no matter what the name. The cost will be little ; the sweeper the
best produced by modern genius. 'Tis a worthy present.

15,000 DEALERS SELL THEM.
BISSELL CARPET SWEEPER CO., GRAND RAPIDS, MICH.
103 CHAMBERS STREET, NEW YORK.

you write, please mention "The Cosmopolitan."

> The Christmas papers now appear,
> The most of them comprising
> A page or two of Christmas cheer
> And stacks of advertising.
>
> —"The Holiday Numbers," from *Pickings
> From Puck*, 1892

Ladies' Blotter Perfumed with HOYT'S GERMAN COLOGNE The Most Fragrant and Lasting of Perfume

1900

PRICE TRIAL SIZE 25¢
MEDIUM SI...

JANUARY

JULY
S. M. T. W. T. F. S.
1 2 3 4 5 6 7
8 9 10 11 12 13 14

OCTOBER
S. M. T. W. T. F.
1 2 3 4 5

A Christmas gift worth having is one that is handsome,
durable and the source of unending enjoyment. Such a
present would be

The Everett Piano

It combines these qualities of a gift with all the requisites
of a first-class piano.

If not for sale by your local dealer, address
THE JOHN CHURCH CO., Cincinnati, O.

"From Andante to Allegro," an illustrated pamphlet, will
be sent free to any one who will mention where this advertisement was seen.

NOW OPEN.
*Grand Christmas
Exhibition
of*
TOYS,
DOLLS, GAMES
and
HOLIDAY
PRESENTS.

Acknowledged to be the
largest and most attractive
Collection of NOVELTIES
ever seen. Direct impor-
tation and lowest prices.

To avoid the great rush
later, our patrons are kindly invited to make their pur-
chases early in the month.

F. A. O. SCHWARZ,
42 E. 14th St. New-York.
CIRCULAR MAILED ON APPLICATION.

MARCH
S. M. T. W. T.

4 5 6 7 8
11 12 13 14 15 16
18 19 20 21 22 23
25 26 27 28 29 30

MANUFACTURED BY
E. W. HOYT & C...
LOWELL, Mas...

RUBIFOAM
FOR THE TEETH

DELICIOUSLY FLAVORED PRICE 25¢ A BOTTLE

COPYRIGHT, 1900.

Holiday windows were an amusement to shoppers and a bonanza to store owners, encouraging the creation of bigger and better displays each year. An 1874 arrangement of dolls in a series of tableaus in Macy's window drew so many spectators that a Christmas window display became an annual tradition. In 1883, many of the figures were set into motion by steam powered mechanisms, and by the 1890s hundreds of mechanical figures performed in Macy's window in a month-long display.

One 1894 Christmas store window featured a constantly revolving panorama that showed in turn wax figures of Solomon and Sheba, Gulliver, Jack the Giant Killer, and other such familiar characters to the crowds that gathered on the street. Sketches of another one, done for *Harper's Young People* in 1881, show multiple tableaus of doll-like figures: a circus scene with horseback rider, a sailor boy, a milkmaid, musicians, a seaside scene, a baby in exquisite christening gown, charity in action, and an impressive Venetian palace setting.

The discovery that pleasing the public during the holidays could result in better sales led manufacturers to offer attractive premiums in time for Christmas—something free to send for with proof of purchase. Many magazines hoped to earn readership loyalty with elaborate holiday editions, and newspapers such as *The Philadelphia Inquirer* published holiday supplements filled with Christmas stories, puzzles, games, and paper dolls to delight the youngest readers.

It is so easy to keep Christmas! There is as much jollity and comfort to the baby in the squeaking duck, which it can immediately slobber so as to cover its hands and face with red paint, as in the most elaborate and exquisite mechanical chariot and horses that roll along the carpet and upset against the harsh-rug. The paper doll is not less welcome than the Paris belle with lace dresses.

—*Harper's Monthly*, 1869

EAGLE BRAND

GAIL BORDEN

A Me...

I wish you a Merry Christmas

Pet wants a doll, does she? She can have one two inches long, or two yards—or any intervening size, and Dolly can have the appointments of a princess—camel hair shawl, diamond necklace, ermine cloak, card-case, photograph album, ivory brush and comb, parasol and Saratoga trunk.
—*Scribner's Monthly*, 1871

Direct from Sonneberg to Pittsburgh.

Aus der
Spielwarenstadt
Sonneberg i/Thueringen.

Children too had gifts to give. Mamas, papas, aunts, and uncles all had to be considered despite a child's lack of money. The solution was an old one—make something yourself! Penwipers were easy and necessary to keep pen nibs from rusting. Pincushions were a necessity for seamstresses of every age. Button bags could be simple or ornate. Photograph frames could be decorated with silk roses or pinecones by the older child. In fact, there were so many projects illustrated in the pages of magazines that a child could be busy nearly forever.

I heard a little girl say, "Well, really, it is queer,
But making Christmas presents keeps me busy all the year!
In January I begin, and long before I'm through
Here comes December, round again, and Christmas with it, too!

—Untitled poem from "Jack-In-The-Pulpit" in *St. Nicholas*, 1887

Grownups made gifts as well—some for the economy of it, some for the personal touch. Fathers labored for weeks on dollhouses or child-sized bedroom suites. Mothers lovingly stitched wardrobes for dolls and knitted warm mittens and caps. Young women embroidered romantic fancies onto gifts made for someone very special.

What time, what thought, what interest were bestowed in the good old Christmas times that are past and gone, on the simple gift for one's best beloved! How one planned and dreamed and worked one's heart's love into the queer, old-fashioned slippers with "his" monogram on the toes! On the dainty blue satin braces with the significant forget-me-nots climbing their way to the shoulder and—fond supposition!—the heart at the same time. How those bits of feminine handiwork were cherished then! And oh! with what covert sneers would they be received in this sordid age and promptly condemned as "fusty old things," to be tossed aside…

—*The Illustrated American*, 1894

58

Peterson's Magazine, December, 1867.

Smoking or Lounging Cap.

Men also received "store-bought" gloves, shaving kits, collar boxes, ties, and tie studs. Women gratefully received silver, glass, and china for their tables, fragile knick-knacks for their parlors, and handkerchiefs, aprons, and jewelry for themselves—whether purchased from the mail-order catalog for under a dollar or from Tiffany's window for a small fortune. For gift-buyers still befuddled, the magazines offered suggestions.

"Many a young girl fairly longs for a pretty party dress, and the amount is put into a piece of jewelry, under the idea that jewelry must be given," *The Ladies' Home Journal* noted in 1893. The fashion pages were full of stylish and costly gowns but for those who were not wealthy, there was a more practical fashion solution. Dry goods stores put fabrics up into gift lengths suitable for a dress that a competent seamstress could make for herself. But whether ready-to-make or ready-to-wear, fabulously expensive or within an average budget, something in the latest vogue was a very wise choice for the person whose job it was to make Christmas complete for everyone—and so deserved to be gifted well.

With
wi
fo

6000

and plenty
e for you
Christmas.

Merr

After 1905, the greeting card became an extension of holiday giving—a way to inexpensively extend wishes to friends, neighbors, and acquaintances. A "golden age" of postcards occurred from about 1906 to the First World War, spawning a collecting mania among children who filled the scrapbooks they received for Christmas with treasured examples. Many cards were printed in Germany with Yuletide images that sometimes reflected old world beliefs. Good luck and prosperity symbols such as horseshoes, four-leaf clovers, and pigs were occasionally featured on both Christmas and New Year cards. Angels were pictured delivering presents, and St. Nicholas was as likely to be seen in his long robes of various colors as Santa Claus. All that mattered to senders were the colorful pictures and appealing subjects—the same qualities that appeal to collectors today.

Wit
every
ngs

The good giver of gifts is the true genius of the season.

—*Harper's Monthly*, 1886

While there's Christmas in the air
Christmas greeting everywhere
I am sending this to you.
Merry Christmas.

A happy Christmas

A Merry Christmas

A Me...

Best Christmas Wishes

A Merry Christmas

A MERRY CHRISTMAS

A merry
Christmas.

Throw wide the door, O soul of mine,
Make glad the heart this Christmas time;
Yea, give to all a merry feast
In word, or look, or smile, at least.

—From *Frank Leslie's Popular
Monthly*, 1893

Hearty
Greetings

XMAS GREETINGS

*A Happy
Christmas*

*Wishing you
A Merry
Christmas*

Merry
Christmas

With dance and song and happy play
ay Yule's glad moments speed away.

Whatever gift was given, large or small, the Victorians knew it must be given from the heart. Love in all its forms has always been the soul of Christmas, and always will be.

COMPLIMENTS OF THE SEASON FROM

MANUFACTURERS' FIRE AND MARINE INSURANCE CO.

OF BOSTON.

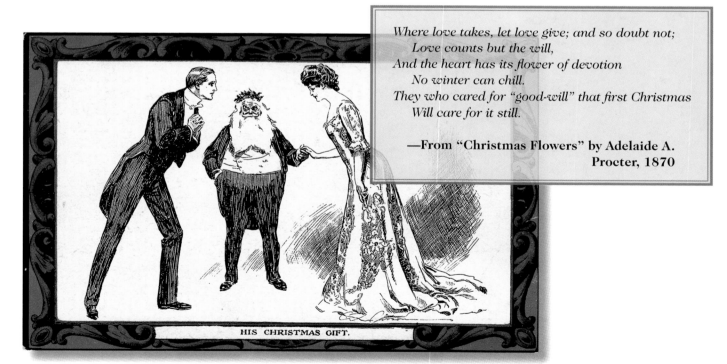

HIS CHRISTMAS GIFT.

Where love takes, let love give; and so doubt not;
 Love counts but the will,
And the heart has its flower of devotion
 No winter can chill.
They who cared for "good-will" that first Christmas
 Will care for it still.

—From "Christmas Flowers" by Adelaide A.
Procter, 1870

Chapter Four
Good Santa Claus

What a wonderful wizard is good Santa Claus!
What a cunning old craftsman is he!
He reads every thought and he speaks every tongue;
He's both man and woman, he's old and he's young.

—**From "Christmas Around The World," by Mar-**
gherita Arlina Hamm, 1896

Santa Claus as we know him today is the product of evolution. He began in the fourth century as Nicholas, Archbishop of Myra—a city in what is now Turkey. Tradition holds that he became the Patron Saint of boys after reviving three murdered schoolboys. He became the Patron Saint of young girls, as well as a symbol of giving, after saving three sisters from a dishonorable future by tossing bags of gold into their window at night to serve as a marriage dowry.

Saint Nicholas of holiday legend dressed in an outfit resembling bishop's robes, sometimes with a bishop's mitre on his head or a hat resembling one. He was somber and lean, no doubt from trudging around through European snows on foot. He carried treats for good children along with switches for the bad, while frequently clutching a fir tree.

As times and religious attitudes changed, so did Saint Nicholas. In England, influenced by the Protestant Reformation, he became Father Christmas. Early German and Scandinavian emigrants to America passed on the name Kris Kringle, probably a misunderstanding of the "Christ Kind" or Christ Child who was believed to bestow Christmas gifts to children in some regions.

Bell-schneckle or Besnickle, named for old-time traveling holiday mummers, was a stand-in for Saint Nicholas among the early Pennsylvania Germans. A member of the community disguised in rough furs, he trekked from cabin to cabin in frontier settlements, gruffly questioning children about their behavior and scattering treats as he left. The name Santa Claus reached America with the New Amsterdam Dutch who adored their fat, jolly "Sinter Klaas" with his pack of good gifts.

Christmas Greetings

OLD FATHER CHRISTMAS

A Merry Christmas

A Merry Christmas

1166.

A Merry Christmas to you

JOSEPH HORNE & CO,
Penn Avenue Stores,
PITTSBURGH

His evolution complete, the latest version of St. Nicholas had been well defined in print by Clement C. Moore when illustrator Thomas Nast showed the world how Santa Claus looked. The rest was in the hands and imaginations of children.

HARPER'S NEW MONTHLY MAGAZINE.

NO. XCI.—DECEMBER, 1857.—VOL. XVI.

A Christmas Garland of American Poems.

[From "THE POETS OF THE NINETEENTH CENTURY." 8vo. Superbly Illustrated. Harper & Brothers.]

A VISIT FROM SAINT NICHOLAS.

CLEMENT C. MOORE.

'TWAS the night before Christmas, when all through the house
Not a creature was stirring, not even a mouse;
The stockings were hung by the chimney with care,
In hopes that St. Nicholas soon would be there;
The children were nestled all snug in their beds,
While visions of sugar-plums danced in their heads;

VOL. XVI.—No. 91.—A

I am no child, yet still I love
Above all saints old Santa Claus;
For he has simmered down to one,
The countless ages' many laws;
"Do Good" is all his testament,
"Be Good" is all that he commands.
He fills the stockings with the seeds
And leaves the fruit to human hands.

—From *The Ladies' World*, 1901

And Mamma in her 'kerchief, and I in my cap,
Had just settled our brains for a long winter's nap;
When out on the lawn there arose such a clatter,
I sprang from the bed to see what was the matter.
Away to the window I flew like a flash,
Tore open the shutters and threw up the sash.
The moon on the breast of the new-fallen snow,
Gave the lustre of mid-day to objects below,
When, what to my wondering eyes should appear,
But a miniature sleigh, and eight tiny rein-deer,
With a little old driver, so lively and quick,
I knew in a moment it must be St. Nick.
More rapid than eagles his coursers they came,
And he whistled, and shouted, and called them by name:
"Now, *Dasher!* now, *Dancer!* now, *Prancer!* and *Vixen!*
On, *Comet!* on, *Cupid!* on, *Donder* and *Blitzen!*
To the top of the porch! to the top of the wall!
Now dash away! dash away! dash away all!"
As dry leaves that before the wild hurricane fly,
When they meet with an obstacle, mount to the sky;
So up to the house-top the coursers they flew,
With the sleigh full of toys, and St. Nicholas too.
And then, in a twinkling, I heard on the roof,
The prancing and pawing of each little hoof—
As I drew in my head, and was turning around,
Down the chimney St. Nicholas came with a bound.
He was dressed all in fur from his head to his foot,
And his clothes were all tarnished with ashes and soot;
A bundle of toys he had flung on his back,
And he looked like a peddler just opening his pack.
His eyes—how they twinkled! his dimples how merry!
His cheeks were like roses, his nose like a cherry!
His droll little mouth was drawn up like a bow,
And the beard of his chin was as white as the snow;
The stump of a pipe he held tight in his teeth,
And the smoke it encircled his head like a wreath;
He had a broad face and a little round belly,
That shook, when he laughed, like a bowlful of jelly.
He was chubby and plump, a right jolly old elf,
And I laughed when I saw him, in spite of myself;
A wink of his eye and a twist of his head,
Soon gave me to know I had nothing to dread;
He spoke not a word, but went straight to his work,
And filled all the stockings; then turned with a jerk,
And laying his finger aside of his nose,
And giving a nod, up the chimney he rose;
He sprang to his sleigh, to his team gave a whistle,
And away they all flew like the down of a thistle.
But I heard him exclaim, ere he drove out of sight,
"Happy Christmas to all, and to all a good-night!"

December Santa Claus shall bring—
Of happy children happy king,
Who with his sleigh and rein-deer stops
At all good people's chimney-tops.

—From "December," by Frank Dempster in
***St. Nicholas,* 1887**

A Blissful Christmas

A Merry Christmas

Christmas Greeting

Workshop of Santa Claus 1873

Santa Claus was a big, jolly fellow in fur who loved children and who, unseen and mysterious, came once a year with a sleigh and reindeer to bring real things—the very things they wanted most. His sleigh traveled through the air and over the housetops. He could come down a chimney of any size with his pack, and he always did come, and the long stockings that the little boy and his sister hung, one at each corner of the mantle over the fireplace, were always filled.
—"A Christmas Memory," 1899

Happy Christmas

A Happy Christmas

Santa brings a pack of cheer
For Christmas and the coming year.

Wishing you Christmas Cheer

A MERRY XMAS

SISTER'S DELIGHT

A Merry Christmas

Here I come to wish you

A MERRY CHRISTMAS

Just when Santa, under all his names, had evolved nicely into a persona to please everyone, the world began to change, along with its demands on him. There were more people moving further and faster, and the gifts that children yearned for were becoming increasingly complex.

They want electric playthings
*   That sting you where you touch,*
With photographic wonders,
*   And cameras and such.*

—**"The Wail Of Santa Claus," 1899**

CHRISTMAS GREETINGS
If it doesn't snow, there's no need to complain
For Santa can come in his aeroplane. · · · ·

They say that Santa this year goes
A'round the town in the same old clothes
For as he has to keep strictly his dates
He uses an auto now for his
Precious
    Freights.

So Santa was asked once more to adapt, since adaptation is the key to evolution. When necessary he arrived by train, or automobile, or aeroplane. His presents became more mechanized and technical, with just enough magic to gladden children's hearts.

CHRISTMAS CHEER

Santa Claus, dear old Saint, simply brings into the home each year a new era of good will all round, and when children find as they do that he had no tangible existence as a man, they accept him the more intelligently as an angel.
—Margaret Sangster, 1900

Santa Claus's Letter of Thanks

Christmas Wish

Xmas Greetings

Chapter Five
Thrice Welcome Christmas

Now thrice welcome, Christmas;
Which brings us good cheer,
Minced pies and plum porridge,
Good ale and strong beer.

—Poor Robin's Almanac, 17th century

HEAVEN BLESS YOU MERRY GENTLEFOLK
LET NOTHING YOU DISMAY

'Tis gentle good Humour
makes Life sweet.
To Wish You
a Right Merry
Christmas

A MERRY CHRISTMAS

Christmas bells
across the snow,
Mistletoe and holly,
Bear the Christmas
message.

Christmas
comes but once a
year, its my duty
to greet you dear;
May all blessings
of this loving day,
make you feel
most happy and gay.

December
25

A MERRY
CHRISTMAS

912

MAY YOU AND YOU

XMAS
GREETINGS

A HAPPY CHRISTMAS

Only the Fourth of July was as happy as Christmas. It was as though the human heart could not quietly contain its exuberance. Before the explosions of mirth and joy on Christmas Day, however, there came a night of shared devotion for many families—a night of quiet intimacy and hopeful expectation, whether spent in church or around the home hearth. Others attended parties to fill the evening hours with a sense of good fellowship and fun.

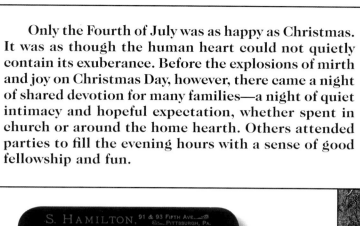

Then be ye glad, good people, this night of all the year;
And light ye up your candles, his star it shineth near.
And all in Earth and Heaven our Christmas Carol sing.
"Goodwill and peace and glory," and all the bells shall ring!

—From "Christmas Carols," in *Frank Leslies' Chatterbox*, 1881

Christmas Greetings

PEACE ON EARTH

O morning stars, together
Proclaim the holy birth;
And praises sing to
God the King,
And peace to men on earth.

Bishop Phillips Brooks

SERIES 409

Carols were originally meant to be danced as well as sung, an enjoyable activity that became far too secular through time. In place of the boisterous troupes that once performed for food, drink, or a few pennies, singers of purely Yuletide songs went round with good wishes (and some remaining expectations of refreshment). In England, there were "waits" before there were carolers, members of the poor or serving class hoping for the charity of the wealthy they serenaded. In America, carols were sung as joyously around the home parlor organ or piano as in the churches or the streets.

Never let any Christmas pass that you do not sing the dear old Christmas songs. Somebody at the piano, everybody singing and the whole gamut of praise and melody weaving itself around the day…
—Margaret Sangster, 1900

83

Often the tree wasn't decorated until Christmas Eve, after all the little ones had been tucked into bed. For them, it had been a day of happy anticipation that culminated in the all-important rite of hanging stockings on the fireplace mantle—anticipation that was revived in dreams of sugarplums and toys and a jolly old elf.

There was just one Santa Claus, and there was no faith and no feeling quite like that on the afternoon before Christmas, when he drove the tack into the back left corner of the mantle piece and hung on it his longest and reddest stocking, and then sat in different parts of the room to look at it and so make sure that Santa Claus could not fail to see it first thing.

—"A Christmas Memory," 1899

It was Christmas Eve! From many a church tower the bells were chiming with a musical monotone, bearing far away into the echoes the tidings of the anniversary. The moon was clear and bright; the snow lay in white hard masses over roads and walks, and the merry jingle of the sleigh-bells sounded on the night air.
—Annie S. Frost, 1867

CHRISTMAS GREETINGS

Bright be your Christmas

Perhaps in their dreams children heard the bells or were awakened by them, because bells were an integral part of Christmas. They called people to church and sent them on their way home again. For centuries, English churches sounded the "Devil's Knell" or "Old Lad's Passing" at midnight of Christmas Eve, giving notice to Satan of his doom. Long believed to drive away evil influences, bells cleared the air for the holy birth. They also loudly announced it was Christmas Day as they clamorously pealed in the morning.

And all the bells on earth shall ring
On Christmas Day, on Christmas Day;
And all the angels in heaven shall sing,
On Christmas Day in the morning.

—Old English carol

"...long before daylight, long before
the fires were lit; to race out into the sitting room and back with the stuffed, lumpy
stocking—this was the one great joy worth
the whole year of waiting."
—"A Christmas Memory," 1899

Christmas morning in the American South was
sheer bedlam. Children and servants raced each other
to be "first foot" into each bedchamber, calling out
for and claiming a gift in exchange for their greetings. There was a tooting of tin horns, a rattling of
toy drums, a booming of guns and cannons, and the
unmistakable splutter of firecrackers. Only when
everyone had gathered in the living room, dressed in
their best clothing, did the cacophony abate.

Once the family was roused—however they were roused—it was time to gather around the tree, where something wonderful waited for everyone.

A Merry Christmas.

Christmas Greetings

A Happy Christmas

With joys, the gayest of the gay,
May dear old Father Christmas call
On you and yours, on Christmas Day,
And bid you welcome to them all!
S. R. Cowan. M. A.

On Merry, Merry Christmas
   Gladdest day of all the year,
Let all our hearts be joyful
   With the little children dear.

　　　—Trade card, c.1883

91

The next order of business was breakfast, and after that, preparation for the coming guests. Mother and the girls had food to cook and the Christmas table to set. Father and the boys went outside to clear the walkways and have some fun as the visitors started arriving.

A Merry Christmas to You

FOR X MA

IN THE MORNING.

The beaten paths crinkled beneath the tread of pedestrians and the runners of sleighs; men's breath congealed in fanciful frost-work upon their comforters and coat collars; boys at work, knee deep in drifts, shoveling new paths or clearing the pure snow from steps and walks, found it inconvenient to pelt each other, from the inadhesiveness of the material, but made it up in shouting Merry Christmas lustily to every passer-by!

—G. W. Haskins, 1850

Christmas Greetings.

Families gathered from near and far; some from such a distance they stayed over for days. Friends and neighbors dropped by as well, usually after dinner when spirits were at their highest. At times it seemed that everyone was out going somewhere, and who was at home to receive them all was a mystery.

Leigh Hunt once wrote that a Christmas Day, to be perfect, should be "clear and cold, with holly-branches in berry, a blazing fire, a dinner with mince-pies, and games and forfeits in the evening." The Victorian hostess tried to provide it all and more, no matter the size of the table or gathering. To accomplish this, she began days ahead to prepare for Christmas dinner and planned the most impressive menu she could.

Christmas Dinner Menu—Raw oysters served with sliced lemon; turtle soup; baked fresh fish; roast turkey garnished with fried oysters, mashed potatoes, Lima beans, pickled beets, mayonnaise of chicken salad, celery, cranberry sauce; Christmas plum pudding with rich sauce; mince pie, sponge and lady cake mixed, fruit and nuts.
—*Practical Housekeeping*, 1881

From Virginia baked ham to barbecued shoat, pork in its many forms was the choice of entree in the American South. *The Delineator* noted that quite a few New England families adhered to the old custom of eating turkey on Christmas Day, while others preferred a pair of well-roasted ducks. Still others thought Christmas incomplete without the traditional English goose.

Stuffing for any toothsome bird brought to the Christmas table could be made with a number of ingredients: bread (with plenty of sage), cornbread, potatoes both plain and sweet, rice, oysters, sausage, chestnuts, walnuts, pecans, prunes and—for the very German taste—sauerkraut.

Roasted Goose

Fill with the following dressing:
2 cupfuls of hot mashed potatoes
4 small onions minced fine
4 tablespoons of sweet cream
1 teaspoonful each of salt, powdered sage,
    sweet marjoram, and chopped parsley
1/4 teaspoon black pepper
the yolks of two eggs

—*The Ladies' World*, 1901

Mince pies, made with spices from the exotic East, were thought to be symbolic of the gifts brought by the Magi. This Christmas pie was so valued that in olden times it was guarded all night to prevent theft.

Mincemeat

Six pounds of currants, three pounds of raisins stoned, three pounds of apples chopped fine, four pounds of suet, two pounds of sugar, two pounds of beef, the peel and juice of two lemons, a pint of sweet wine, a quarter of a pint of brandy, half an ounce of mixed spice. Press the whole into a deep pan when well mixed.
—*Godey's Lady's Book,* 1867

Without the door let sorrow lie;
And if for cold it hap to die,
We'll bury't in Christmas pie,
And evermore be merry.
—Harper's Monthly, 1865

For toasting the day there was only one traditional drink that would do—eggnog—and every competent hostess owned a prized recipe.

Old Virginia Egg Nog

This famous decoction of old Virginia is made of twelve eggs, four glasses of gin, five of brandy, four of sherry and two cups of sugar. The liquor is poured on the yolks of the eggs and the sugar, which are beaten together till thoroughly mixed. Then are added the whites of the eggs, well beaten, and milk enough until the taste is agreeable.

—*Good Housekeeping*, 1900

The most anxiously awaited feature of the Victorian Christmas dinner was the plum pudding, sometimes served with a brandy sauce, sometimes set ablaze, and always topped with holly.

Hallo! A great deal of steam! The pudding was out of the copper. A smell like a washing-day! That was the cloth. A smell like an eating-house, and a pastry cook's next door to each other, with a laundress's next door to that! That was the pudding.
—Charles Dickens, "A Christmas Carol"

Christmas Plum Pudding

A pound of suet, cut in pieces not too fine, a pound of currants, and a pound of raisins stoned, four eggs, half a grated nutmeg, an ounce of citron and lemon-peel, shred fine, a teaspoonful of beaten ginger, half a pound of bread-crumbs, half a pound of flour, and a pint of milk; beat the eggs first, add half the milk, beat them together, and by degrees stir in the flour, then the suet, spice and fruit, and as much milk as will mix it together very thick; then take a clean cloth, dip in boiling water, and squeeze dry. Put in the pudding, tie it down very tightly and closely, boil at least five hours, and serve with brandy sauce.
—*Godey's Lady's Book*, 1867

TOO GOOD TO FLOAT — NOT AIR, BUT SOAP.
COAL OIL JOHNNY'S PETROLEUM SOAP
5 CENTS PER CAKE.

HOLIDAY COMPLIMENTS OF
Jos. Horne & Co.'s
RETAIL STORES,
197, 199 & 20t Penn Ave.
Pittsburg, Pa.

A MERRY CHRISTMAS & A HAPPY NEW YEAR

With Christmas dinner over, attention once more turned to the tree, where small surprises and confections still hid among the branches for little guests—candies in pretty papers, candies in clever toy-like boxes, candies in colorful cornucopias. "A machine in New York is at work turning out every minute three hundred cornucopias, used for putting up candies," *Harpers Bazar* reported in November of 1880—a prodigious effort to meet Christmas needs. Recalling his own boyhood during the shortages of the Civil War, author Hamlin Garland said that a small toy or two and candy were enough to assure a happy holiday. "Christmas would be empty and a hollow mockery without candy and nuts," he wrote.

" OPEN YOUR MOUTH AND SHUT YOUR EYES,
AND IN YOUR MOUTH YOU'LL FIND A PRIZE."

COMPLIMENTS O
Dimling & Over,
→Manufacturin
Confectioners,←

At Christmas play, and make good cheer;
For Christmas comes but once a year.

—Attributed to Thomas Tusser

Wishing you a happy Christmas

Next there were games, followed by music and, if there was room, dancing. There were very old games, such as Blindman's Buff, Forfeits, and Snapdragon. There were newer games too, that Mother found described in her holiday magazines. All were fun and some were played by the grownups as well, for as Mr. Dickens said, "it is good to be children sometimes, and never better than at Christmas, when its mighty Founder was a child himself."

"New England Christmas Home Scenes, and Christmas Games."

Bran Pie

The presents wrapped in paper are put into a large pan and the spaces between them filled with bran or sawdust. The top is covered with piecrust, which is browned in the oven, provided none of the presents can be injured by heat. Another way is to make the top of the pie of thick, brown paper. When set on the table, part of the crust is removed and the presents are taken, one by one, out of the bran.
—*The Young Folks' Cyclopedia*, 1899

The Christmas Bag

Make a large bag of thin white paper—silver paper will do; fill it with sugar plums and tie a string around the top to keep it fast. Then suspend it from the ceiling, or from a large door-frame, and provide a long, light stick. Each player is blindfolded in turn and the stick put into her hand. She is then led within reach of the bag, and told to strike it. If she succeeds in her aim, and tears a hole in it, the sugar plums are scattered on the floor and the little ones scramble for them…Each player is allowed three trials.
—*Godey's Lady's Book,*
1873

Also played at Halloween, Snapdragon was one of the oldest of Christmas games. By today's standards it was a dangerous and foolhardy invitation to disaster. One flaming raisin dropped carelessly onto clothing or carpeting could lead to tragedy. More than a few Victorian games and toys were surprisingly hazardous, however, and the miracle is that so many children survived unhurt. Never try this game with either children or adults.

Snap-Dragon

A dish of raisins being prepared, some heated brandy or spirits of wine is poured over the fruit, and then set on fire, the other lights in the room being extinguished. The young folks then stand round the dish to pluck out the lighted raisins and eat them as hastily as they can, but rarely without warming their hands and mouths.

—*The Boys Treasury Of Sports, Pastimes, And Recreations,* 1854

As described by Dickens in "A Christmas Carol," both Forfeits and Blind Man's Buff (or Bluff) were favorite games with both old and young, and it was difficult to say which group enjoyed them more. Forfeits were a kind of penance paid for losing or breaking rules in a previous game. Forfeits suggested in the 1899 *Young Folks' Cyclopedia Of Games And Sports* included:

1. Blow out a candle as it is passed rapidly back and forth before the mouth.
2. Laugh in one corner of the room, sing in another, cry in the third, and whistle in the fourth.
3. Bow to the prettiest person in the room, kneel to the wittiest, and kiss the one you love best.
4. Pay a compliment to each person in the room.
5. Kiss your shadow.
6. Answer "no" to a question from each of the company.
—*The Young Folks' Cyclopedia,* 1899

Santa visits You to-day,
May he bring good cheer,
Peace, Content,
and Merriment for
the coming Year.

FRAUD ON THE FACE OF IT.

MISS PASSAY. — Oh, you naughty man! It is n't fair! I do believe you can see!

Blind Man's Buff

A game played by any number of persons, one of whom is blindfolded by tying a handkerchief over his eyes. The object of the blind-man is to catch one of the others. If he guesses correctly the name of the one caught, that one must take his place as blind-man; if he guess incorrectly, he must try to catch someone else. The players usually try to mislead the blind-man and turn his attention in various ways.

A Merry Christmas

The New England Christmas celebration Harriet Martineau described in 1835 followed games with dancing. "By ten o'clock," she wrote, "all were well warmed for the ride home with steaming mulled wine, and the prosperous evening closed with shouts of mirth." Little had changed by the end of the Victorian era in terms of hospitality. Visitors were less likely to stay a week or more but they were as cordially entertained and as hospitably sent on their way, a mulled wine or a hot toddy under their belts for warmth.

Christmas Day was over, and most would agree that it was all they had hoped for in early December when the holidays seemed merely a bright promise. "The memory of such a season should always sparkle and brighten with the joyous, the generous, the beneficent and the good," *Appleton's Journal* declared in 1870.

But some must have wondered whether it could ever be as good again without realizing that generations before them had asked the same question. The country had suffered growing pains in many forms, even a devastating Civil War, and yet managed to revive the Yuletide spirit each December 25th. In the third quarter of the nineteenth century, a wave of scientific discovery infected the Christmas celebration with growing skepticism, and yet still it survived

"Christmas is in the air, in the mind, in the heart," wrote the editor of *Harper's Monthly* in 1869. "It makes no difference whether we are ten or fifty, whether we hang up our stockings or are ourselves Santa Claus, the holiday feeling descends upon us all, and a sense of feast and festival goes with us as we go, and assures us that the chimes duly ring, although we may be a little too far away—who said deaf?—to hear."

I send you my Love and some Holly To help make your Christmas Day Jolly.

A Merry Christmas

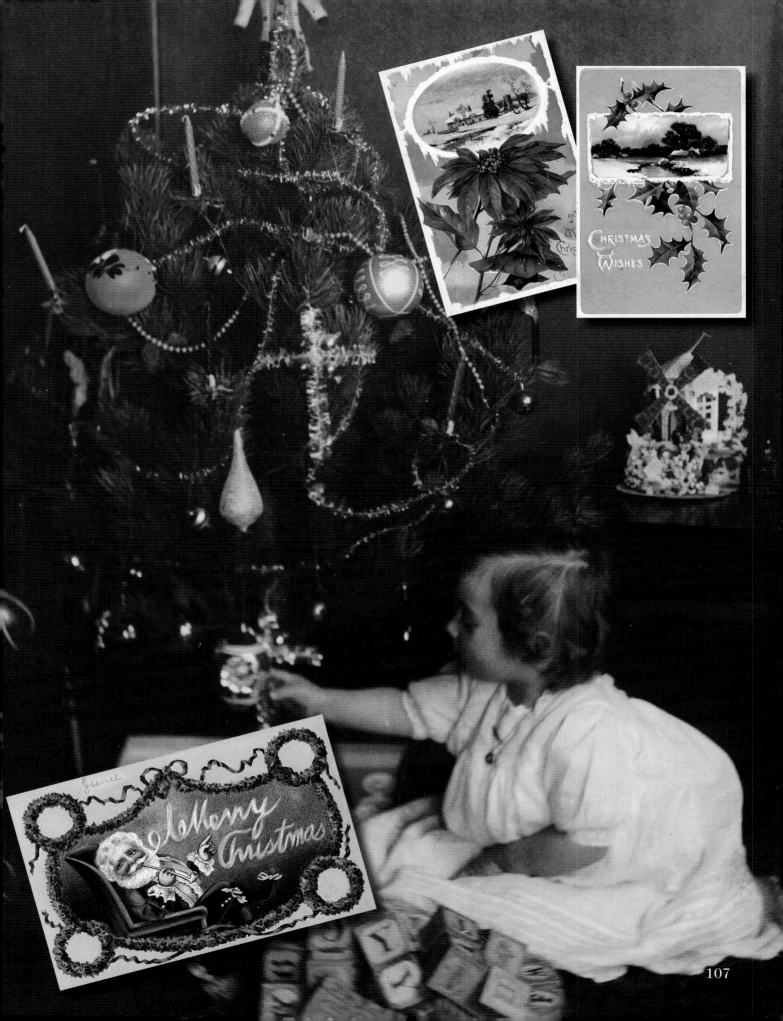

CHRISTMAS WISHES

Merry Christmas

Bibliography

Appleton's Journal, 1 January 1870.

Barber, Mrs. M. L. "Christmas Decorations." *The Ladies' Home Journal*, December 1893.

Barrows, Anna. "Christmas Greens." *Good Housekeeping*, 26 December 1885.

"Books And Authors At Home." *Scribner's Monthly Magazine*, January 1870.

The Boy's Treasury Of Sports, Pastimes, And Recreations. New York: Clark, Austin & Smith, 1854.

Buday, George. *The History of the Christmas Card*. England: Spring Books, 1954.

Champlin, John D., and Arthur Bostwick. *The Young People's Cyclopedia of Games and Sports*. New York: Henry Holt And Company, 1899.

Childs, George W. "My Christmas As A Boy." *The Ladies' Home Journal*, December 1893.

"The Children's Carol." *The Illustrated American*, Christmas 1894.

"Christmas Ceremonies." *Appleton's Journal*, 31 December 1870.

"Christmas In Yorkshire." *Appleton's Journal*, 31 December 1870.

"Christmas Notes." *Appleton's Journal*, 31 December 1870.

"Christmas Sports." *The Ladies' Companion*, January 1842.

Coffin, Tristram P. *The Book Of Christmas Folklore*. New York: The Seabury Press, 1973.

Conway, M. D. "The Sacred Flora." *Harper's New Monthly Magazine*, November 1870.

Cooke, John Easton. "An Old Virginian." *Scribner's Monthly Magazine*, July 1881.

Coombs, Edith I., Editor. "Harriet Martineau." *America Visited*, n.d.

The Cosmopolitan, December 1909.

"Culture And Progress Abroad." *Scribner's Monthly Magazine*, April 1871.

Curtis, George William. "Christmas." *Harper's New Monthly Magazine*, December 1883.

Dickens, Charles. "A Christmas Carol." *The Complete Works of Charles Dickens in Sixteen Volumes*. Philadelphia: The Gebbie Publishing Company, Ltd., 1895.

Dickens, Charles. "A Christmas Tree." *Appleton's Journal*, 31 December 1870.

"Editor's Easy Chair." *Harper's New Monthly Magazine*, January 1856.

"Editor's Easy Chair." *Harper's New Monthly Magazine*, February 1868.

"Editor's Easy Chair." *Harper's New Monthly Magazine*, January 1869.

"Editor's Easy Chair." *Harper's New Monthly Magazine*, December 1882.

"Etiquette." *The Ladies' World*, November 1899.

Fales, Winifred. "Home-Made Boxes for Christmas Candies." *The Delineator*, December 1906.

Feune, Lady. "What Christmas Means To Queen Victoria." *The Ladies' Home Journal*, December 1896.

Frank Leslies' *Popular Monthly*, December 1892.

Frazer, James George. *The Golden Bough*. New York: MacMillan Company, 1922.

Frost, S. Annie. "Christmas Eve." *Godey's Lady's Book And Magazine*, December 1867.

"Games For Holiday Evenings." *Godey's Lady's Book And Magazine*, December 1873.

Garland, Hamlin. "A Pioneer Christmas." *The Ladies' Home Journal*, December 1893.

"Getting Ready For Christmas." *The Youth's Companion*, 22 November 1900.

"Godey's Arm-Chair." *Godey's Lady's Book And Magazine*, December 1867.

"Godey's Arm-Chair." *Godey's Lady's Book And Magazine*, December 1873.

Gordon-Sutherland, Helen. "The Christmas Goose and Plum Pudding." *The Delineator*, December 1906.

Hamilton, Dr. Alexander, edited by Robert Micklus. *The History of the Ancient and Honorable Tuesday Club*. Chapel Hill And London: The University Of North Carolina Press, 1990.

Harland, Marion. *When Grandmamma Was New: The Story Of A Virginia Childhood*. Boston: Lothrop Publishing Company, 1899.

Haskins, G. W. "The Ingle Nook." *Godey's Lady's Book And Magazine*, December 1850.

Hillis, Reverend Newell Dwight. "Just Christmas." *The Cosmopolitan*, January 1910.

"Home and Society." *Scribner's Monthly Magazine*, January 1871.

"Home and Society." *Scribner's Monthly Magazine*, January 1872.

"Home and Society." *Scribner's Monthly Magazine*, December 1875.

Hooper, Emma M. "Christmas In The Shops." *The Ladies' Home Journal*, December 1893.

Hower, Ralph M. *History of Macy's of New York 1858-1919*. Massachusetts: Harvard University Press, 1943.

Hornung, Clarence P., Editor. *An Old Fashioned Christmas In Illustration & Decoration*. New York: Dover Publications, Inc., 1975.

Hottes, Alfred Carl. *1001 Christmas Facts and Fancies*. New York: A. T. De La Mare Company, Inc., 1938.

"The Housekeeper." *The Ladies' World*, December 1899.

Hull, Georgiana. "The Fashion." *Good Housekeeping*, 26 December 1885.

Hunt, Leigh. "A Perfect Christmas." *Appleton's Journal*, 31 December 1870.

Irving, Washington. *Old Christmas*. Philadelphia: Henry Altemus Company, c.1896.

"Jack-In-The-Pulpit." *St. Nicholas*, December 1887.

McClellan, Elisabeth. *Historic Dress In America 1607-1870*. New York: Benjamin Blom, Inc., 1904.

McCormick, Eliot. "The New Orleans Christmas Tree." *Harper's Young People*, 6 January 1885.

McWhorter, George C. "The Holidays." *Harper's New Monthly Magazine*, January 1866.

Megee, Katherine E. "Some Virginia Christmas Dishes." *The Ladies' World*, December 1901.

Moffet, Cleveland. "The Pathos Of A City Street At Christmastide." *The Illustrated American*, Christmas 1894.

Munro, Kirk. "Santa Claus Mistake." *Harper's Young People*, 6 January 1885.

"The Old Cabinet." *Scribner's Monthly Magazine*, January 1874.

"Our Christmas At The Pines." *Harper's New Monthly Magazine*, December 1857.

Owen, Catherine. "Home-made Christmas Confections." *Good Housekeeping*, 26 December 1885.

"The Philadelphia Inquirer Christmas Book." Supplement to *The Philadelphia Inquirer*, 24 December 1899.

Plumstead, Mrs. M. J. "Arranging For Christmas." *Good Housekeeping*, 26 December 1885.

Practical Housekeeping. Ohio: The Buckeye Publishing Co., 1881.

Procter, Adelaide A. "Christmas Flowers." *Appleton's Journal*, 31 December 1870.

"Receipts, Etc." *Godey's Lady's Book And Magazine*, December 1867.

Sangster, Margaret E. "Talks With Fathers And Mothers." *Good Housekeeping*, December 1900.

"Sayings And Doings." *Harper's Bazar*, 27 November 1880.

Shepherd, Dorothy. "A Christmas Message." *The Ladies' World*, December 1899.

Spencer, O. M. "Christmas Throughout Christendom." *Harper's New Monthly Magazine*, December 1872.

Stall, Sylvanus, D. D. *With The Children On Sundays*. Philadelphia: The Uplift Publishing Company, 1911.

Swift, Sara D. "Holly and Mistletoe." *The Ladies' World*, December 1899.

"Table-Talk." *Appleton's Journal*, 31 December 1870.

Tabor, Wilhelmina L. "The Housekeeper." *The Ladies' World*, December 1901.

Tennant, Eugenia L. *American Christmases From the Puritans To The Victorians*. New York: Exposition Press, 1973.

"Topics Of The Time." *The Century Magazine*, December 1906.

Train, Arthur Jr. *The Story of Everyday Things*. New York: Harper & Brothers Publishers, 1941.

Turner, Alice H. "Christmas In The old South." *Good Housekeeping*, December 1900.

Walsh, William S. *Curiosities of Popular Customs & of Rites, Ceremonies, Observances, & Miscellaneous Antiquities*. London: J. B. Lippincott Company, 1902.

"A Winter In The South." *Harper's New Monthly Magazine*, August 1858.

Index Of Quotes and Illustrations
With Value Guide

This index identifies the quotes and images used in the book. Where dates are known they are given. Where dates are uncertain, they are suggested with a circa designation. Illustration values have been assigned to reflect the range of prices you might realistically expect to see for these items in shops, shows, and at fleatiques. Be aware that condition is always an important factor that can affect values by as much as 80%.

Unframed illustrations removed from books and magazines are worth little unless of a particularly sought-after topic or by a noted artist. Quality early photographs of Christmas trees or costumed Santas are very desirable and are priced accordingly. The value of advertising trade cards is determined by im-age, topic, product, and size. Die-cut "scrap" pieces of Santas, angels, etc. are wonderful, but the market has been hurt by a flood of reproductions.

Christmas postcards of the pre-World War I era are plentiful and only certain types are pricey. Santas often top this list, especially if pictured full length in a color other than red. Rarities, such as mechanicals and hold-to-lights, can be shockingly costly. "Signed" artist cards by popular illustrators are valued according to quality and scarcity of image. Superior work and popular topics always command more money, while common cards—and you'll quickly learn which these are by browsing the boxes at a weekend fleatique—will be lucky to bring a dollar.

Title Page: Postcard, Santa with finger beside nose, c.1910. $5-7; Trade card, girl with flowers, Beck & Myer, c.1883. $1-2; Postcard, woman in floral hat with poinsettias, c.1910. $3-6; Postcard, boy in blue with holly, c.1908. $2-3; Scrap St. Nicholas, England, c.1906. $12-15.

Contents: Silk fringed greeting card, bird with rose, c.1883. $2-3; Postcard, angel at window, Germany, c.1908. $2-4; Postcard, St. Nicholas with treats for girl, c.1908. $8-14; Postcard, girl in red at window, c.1909. $1-2; Scrap angel with mica accents, c.1896. $15-18.

Introduction: Stereocard, "Anticipation," a young couple visualize Christmas future, Underwood and Underwood, 1901. $5-8.

Page 5: Lines from Spenser's "The Faerie Queen"; Trade card, Seeley Perfumes calendar, 1892. $3-5; Postcard, figure in red and angel at fire, c.1910. $3-4; Trade card, girl in light green coat, no imprint, c.1888. $2-3; Trade card, woman in green, Acme Soap, 1891. $5-8; Trade card, children and geese in snow, no imprint, c.1890. $2-3.

Page 6: Lines from "The Happiest Christmas," by Margaret J. Preston, c.1885; Fireplace scene by C. D. Weldon from *Harper's Young People*, 1885. *Under $5.*

Page 7: Lines from "Winter" by George Johnson, 1850; Trade card, wintry house with child in foreground, Dr. McLane's Liver Pills, c.1887. $2-4; Trade card, sailor at sea, Woolson Spice Company, c.1891. $4-8; Trade card, wintry house, Dr. McLane's Pills, c.1887. $2-4; Trade card, girls at snowy door, Arbuckle's Coffee, c.1890. $2-4.

Page 8: Postcard, wintry scene, c.1911. $1; Trade card, snowy building in leaf, Dayton Spice Mills, c.1887. $1-3; Trade card, house near stream, Capital Coffee, c.1890. $2-3; Trade card, person near wintry gate, c.1888. $2-3; Silk-fringed greeting, horses pulling log, c.1880. $4-6.

Page 9: Memory of a Southern girl as printed in *Historic Dress In America* by Elisabeth McClellan, 1904; Hand-colored fashion plate from *Godey's Lady's Book* for December 1873. $10-15; Postcard, woman in white with holly by H. A. Weiss, c.1912. $7-10.

Page 10: Trade card, girl in stripes, no imprint, c.1885. $2-4; Photograph, toddler in long winter coat, c.1895. $3-5; Postcard, children in snow, c.1908.

$2-4; Photograph, girl in fringed winter coat, c.1903. $3-5; Postcard, girl in red with plumed hat, 1906. $3-5; Photograph, two girls in fur-trimmed coats, c.1905 $5-8; Lines from "Good Cheer" by Charles Edward Barns.

Page 11: Postcard, girls with tree at doorway, c.1908. $3-5; Greeting card, girl and boy, Raphael Tuck & Sons, c.1890. $8-10; Trade card, two girls in pink and tan, Chadwick's Spool Cotton, c.1889. $4-6; Illustration with poem, "My First Muff" by F. C. from *Harper's Young People*, 1881. Under $3.

Page 12: Illustration and poem, "Pinafore Rhymes" by Kate Greenaway, from *Harper's Young People*, 1881. Under $5; Greeting card, girl in green coat and bonnet, c.1903. $2-4; Trade card, girl with muff and toys, Rhodes' Candies, c.1890. $3-5; Postcard, woman in red with skates, 1912. $2-4; Illustration, "The Winter Walk" from *Peterson's Magazine*, 1867. Under $5.

Page 13: Illustration, "Something In The Way" by Jessie McDermott, from *Harper's Young People*, 1881. Under $5.

Page 14: Postcard, boy in blue, Stecher Litho. Co., c.1916. $2-4; Trade card, girl throws snowball, Dr. Ingham's Pills, c.1896. $3-5; Postcard, girl on snowshoes, c.1913. $2-4; Postcard, women in snow fight, Vienne, c.1905. $10-15.

Page 15: Game description from *The Boy's Treasury Of Sports, Pastimes, And Recreations*, 1854; Illustration, "The Tables Turned," for *Harper's Young People*, 1885. Under $5.

Page 16: Postcard, children build snow Santa, Bon Ton Art Co., 1912. $3-5; Postcard, boy and girl with spilled apples, Germany, c.1909. $3-5.

Page 17: Postcard, children build snowman, c.1911. $2-4; Postcard, woman in red with snowballs, by R. Ford Harper, c.1908. $2-4; Trade card, robin snowball ambush, Joseph Horne & Co., c.1900. $3-6.

Page 18: Lines from "Winter," by George Johnson, 1850; Illustration, "On The Wissahickon," from *Godey's Lady's Book*, 1867. Under $6.

Page 19: Postcard, boys skating, c.1907. $1-2; Postcard, people skating and holly, c.1907. $1; Trade card, girl pulled by dog, Peerless Ink Cream, c.1896. $3-6; Trade card, girl skates in green coat, Acme Soap, c.1888. $4-7.

Page 20: Trade card, dog pulled by boy, Ariosa Coffee, c.1889. $3-6; Postcard, boy carries skates, Stecher Litho. Co., c.1913. $2-4; Fashion drawing, skating costume, *Peterson's Magazine*, December 1879. Under $5.

Page 21: Trade card, toboggan, Lutted's Cough Drops, c.1892. $8-12; Postcard, boy coasting, c.1914. $1; Postcard, red-capped boy with sled, c.1914. $2-4; Photograph, boy with sled, c.1890. $12-18; Postcard, boy in white with red sled, c.1912. $2-4.

Page 22: Passage from Harriet Martineau's visit to America, c.1835; Illustration, "Coasting Sketches," by F. S. Church for *Harper's Young People*, 1881. Under $5.

Page 23: Lines from "A Merry Christmas," by George Cooper, date unknown; Postcard, girl in red on toboggan, Dennison, c.1905. $3-5; Postcard, holly and coasting, c.1908. $1; Photograph, people on toboggan, c.1897. $5-8; Postcard, girl in red jacket with sled, c.1908. $1-2; Trade card, boy pushes girl on sled, no imprint, c.1891. $5-8; Trade card, turkeys run from sled, John L. Moorhouse Dry Goods, c.1895. $2-3.

Page 24: Lines on sleighing from *Harper's Monthly*, 1854; Trade card, boy on back of sleigh, Successful Farming Publishing Co., c.1917. $5-8; Postcard, holly and sleigh, Nash, c.1910. $1.

Page 25: Lines from "The Sleighers" by N. G. Shepherd, 1861; Postcard, people sitting in sleigh, c.1913. $2-3; Trade card, hare pulling sleigh, Clark's Mile-End Thread, c.1890. $2-4; Postcard, people out sleighing, 1906. $1-2; Photograph, men and sleigh, c.1890. $5-8.

Pages 26-27: Lines from "A Winter Idyl" by Wm. Hamilton Gibson for *Harper's Monthly*, 1880; Illustration, "A Winter Fantasy" by Archie Gunn for *The Illustrated American*, 1894. Under $20.

Page 28: Lines from "Christmas Comes Again" by Elizabeth Stoddard in *Appleton's Journal*, 1870; Postcard, snowy scene in wood frame with holly, c.1910. $1; Postcard, wintry scene with holly, stars, and bell, A. S. Meeker, 1910. $1; Postcard, snowy scene through stone window, E. Nash, 1910. $1.

Page 29: Unattributed lines appearing in *Harper's Monthly*, January 1866; Postcard, women gather greens, Wolf Publishing Co., 1906. $6-10; Postcard, couple hang holly, by Marion Miller, c.1911. $1-2; Postcard, mother and two children, V. K. Vienne, c.1910. $12-16; Postcard, two children gather holly, Gibson Art Co., c.1917. $1-2.

Page 30: Passage from "Our Christmas At The Pines," *Harper's Monthly*, 1857; Illustration, "Preparing Christmas Greens" by T. De Thulstrup in *Harper's Weekly*, 1880, courtesy of the Dover Publications Archives Series. Under $5.

Page 31: Postcard, girls decorate with mistletoe, c.1907. $2-4; Diecut wishbone Christmas tag, c.1890. $3-5; Postcard, woman in ribboned hat, Raphael Tuck & Sons, c.1909. $2-4; Illustration, "Decorating The Church For Christmas," by F. Dielman for *Harper's Monthly*, 1882. Under $5; Postcard, children with greens come in door, by Ellen H. Clapsaddle, International Art Co., 1912. $8-15.

Page 32: Lines from "The Mistletoe" by Hone in *Harper's Monthly*, 1866; Illustration, "A Christmas Errand," by Pruett Sharr for *The Illustrated American*, 1894. Under $10.

Page 33: Gift tag, holly, Raphael Tuck & Sons, c.1910. $1-3; Postcard, winter scene in circle with holly, Nash Publishing, 1910. $1; Postcard, holly girl, c.1910. $4-7; Postcard, holly boy, by Ellen H. Clapsaddle, S. Garre Pub., 1909. $10-16; Postcard, woman in blue with holly, by Hamilton King, c.1909. $6-10.

Page 34: Lines from "A Christmas Thought" in *Harper's Monthly*, 1882; Postcard, winter scene with holly, c.1907. $1; Postcard, woman in red with holly, c.1908. $2-3; Postcard, girl in blue circle with holly, c.1908. $2-3; Postcard, girl in pink in gold circle with holly, c.1908. $2-3.

Page 35: Passage from "Getting Ready For Christmas," *The Youth's Companion*, 1900; Postcard, woman in red, hand-colored, c.1909. $4-6; Postcard, woman in blue, c.1910. $2-4; Postcard, woman in white with holly, c.1910. $2-4; Postcard, winter scene in gold crescent, Robbins Pub., 1907. $1.

Page 36: Lines by Charles MacKay appearing in *1001 Christmas Facts and Fancies* by Alfred Carl Hottes, 1938; Postcard, woman and holly on a silver ground, c.1909. $4-8; Postcard, woman in red vest, c.1904. $3-6; Postcard, woman in holly wreath on gold ground, Julius Bien & Co., 1908.

$5-8; Postcard, woman in golden crescent, c.1907. $3-5; Postcard, winter scene in silver frame with holly, c.1909. $1; Postcard, dachshunds upset holly basket, hand colored, c.1908. $8-12.

Page 37: Postcard, woman in poinsettias, hand-colored, The Fairman Co., c.1910. $3-5; Postcard, poinsettias and winter scene, Nash Publishing Co., c.1908. $1; Postcard, lady in lilac hat, c.1909. $4-6; Postcard, poinsettia basket, c.1909. $1.

Page 38: Postcard, woman in white with poinsettias, c.1912. $3-5; Postcard, woman in white with muff, Bergman Co., 1912. $3-5; Postcard, woman in ermine, Bergman Co., 1912. $3-5; Postcard, woman opening box by M. Farini, 1911. $4-6; Postcard, poinsettias and winter scene, E. Nash Co., 1912. $1.

Page 39: St. Winfrid's words from *Curiosities Of Popular Customs*, by Wm. S. Walsh, 1897; Postcard, young people gather Christmas greens, c.1907. $1-2; Trade card, children with tree and dog, Dr. McLane's Liver Pills, c.1890. $3-4; Postcard, child with axe and tree, c.1908. $1-2.

Page 40: Postcard, December 25, angel lighting trees, c.1907. $2-3; Postcard, photo-type, angelic woman and tree, c.1914. $3-6; Postcard, flying angel with tree, c.1909. $2-4.

Page 41: Illustration, "Martin Luther And His Family" from *Harper's Monthly*, 1883. Under $3; Illustration, "Our Christmas Tree," from *Harper's Monthly*, 1858. Under $6.

Page 42: Lines from "The Fashion," by Georgiana Hull, in *Good Housekeeping*, 1885; Postcard, photo-type, family and Christmas tree, Saxony, c.1915. $3-6; Photograph, Christmas tree and gifts, c.1905. $10-12; Postcard, children and Christmas tree, c.1911. $2-4.

Page 43: Photograph, Christmas tree with gifts, c.1912. $10-12; Postcard, children dance around tree, Sander Co., c.1908. $2-4; Photograph, children sitting around tree, c.1910. $10-15; Photograph, Christmas tree in church, c.1910. $4-6; Postcard, family around tree, 1907. $2-4; Postcard, photo-type, couple beside tree, Germany, c.1914. $2-3.

Page 44: Illustration, "The Christmas Celebration At The New Orleans Exposition," by John Durkin for *Harper's Young People*, 1885. Under $5.

Page 45: Lines from "The Dear Old Tree" by Luella Wilson Smith, 1907; Illustration, "The Christmas Tree," by Clara M. Burd in *With The Children on Sunday* by Sylvanus Stall, 1911. $12-20.

Page 46: Lines from "Marmion" by Sir Walter Scott; Trade card, child with mistletoe, McLane's Vermifuge, c.1883. $2-3; Illustration, "Gathering Christmas Mistletoe," *Peterson's Magazine*, 1869. Under $5.

Page 47: Lines from "The Mistletoe" by Hone, 1865; Postcard, mistletoe maid, Julius Bien & Co., 1908. $6-10; Private mailing card, "Mistletoe" by Howard Chandler Christy, 1905. $15-18; Postcard, couple under mistletoe on silver ground, T. P. & Co., c.1907. $3-5.

Page 48: Quote from "Editor's Easy Chair," *Harper's Monthly*, 1855; Postcard, photo-type, woman sitting under mistletoe, Bamforth & Co., 1910. $1-3; Postcard, surprised under the mistletoe, c.1908. $3-6; Postcard, kissed while sleeping, c.1908. $2-4.

Page 49: Print by Harrison Fisher, 1908. $20-30.

Page 50: Lines from "The Sign Of The Christmas Tree" by Pauline Francis Clamp; Postcard, holly leaf girl with snowball, E. Nash Co., c.1908. $6-8; Postcard, holly leaf girl with cornucopia, E. Nash Co., c.1908. $6-8; Postcard, holly leaf girl with gift, E. Nash Co., c.1908. $6-8; Postcard, holly leaf girl with dog, E. Nash Co., c.1908. $6-8.

Page 51: Postcard, girl in green with parcels, Whitney Made, c.1916. $2-4; Postcard, girl in red and blue with tree and parcels, c.1909. $1-3; Postcard, people on snowy street, John Winsch Co., 1914. $1-2; Postcard, girl in green with holly and parcels, 1908. $2-3; Postcard, man and woman with packages, by H. B. Griggs, c.1908. $8-12.

Page 52: Poem, "The Holiday Numbers," from *Pickings From Puck*, 1892; Advertisement for Lundborg's perfumes from *Puck*, 1894. Under $5; Advertisement for Victor Bicycles from *The Cosmopolitan*, 1891. Under $5; Advertising calendar blotter, Hoyt's German cologne, 1900. $15-20; Advertisement for Bissell Carpet Sweeper in *The Cosmopolitan*, 1891. No value; Advertisement for Everett Piano in *The Cosmopolitan*, 1891. No value; Advertisement for F. A. O. Schwarz in *St. Nicholas* magazine, 1887. Under $5.

Page 53: Postcard, mother and boys on city streets, c.1907. $1; Photograph, store window display, c.1907. Rare, $35+.

Page 54: Illustration, "Scenes In Shop Windows," by Jessie McDermott for *Harper's Young People*, 1881. Under $5.

Page 55: Paper doll from *The Philadelphia Inquirer* children's Christmas supplement, 1899. $5-8; Paper doll from *The Philadelphia Inquirer* children's Christmas supplement, 1899. $5-8.

Page 56: Trade card, Borden's Eagle Brand milk, 1896. $4-6; Photograph, tintype, boy on rocking horse, c.1867. $15-18; Photograph, toddler with Christmas toys, c.1907. $15-18; Postcard, boy gives toy soldier to girl, c.1908. $2-4; Postcard, boy with toy soldiers, c.1910. $3-5; Photograph, Christmas gifts, c.1900. $15-18.

Page 57: Quote from the "Home & Society" column of *Scribner's Monthly*, January 1871; Postcard, girl in blue with doll, Raphael Tuck & Sons, c.1910. $2-4; Photograph, girl with bisque head doll, composition body, c.1911. $8-10; Trade card, doll and toy imports from Sonneberg, c.1910. $6-10; Photograph, girl with bisque head doll, cloth or kid body, c.1893. $8-10; Trade card, toddler with doll, no imprint, c.1885. $3-5.

Page 58: Untitled poem from "Jack-In-The-Pulpit" in *St. Nicholas*, 1887; Quote from *The Illustrated American*, 1894; Illustration, "Finishing The Christmas gift," *Harper's Young People*, 1885. $1; Craft project, muff bag, from *Peterson's Magazine*, 1870. No value; Craft project, key basket, from *Peterson's Magazine*, 1889. No value; Craft project, pin cushion, from *The Delineator*, 1895. No value; Craft project, sachet, from *The Delineator*, 1895. No value.

Page 59: Craft project, smoking or lounging cap, from *Peterson's Magazine*, 1867. No value; Craft project, fan wall pocket, from *Peterson's Magazine*, 1889. No value; Advertisement for holiday gown from *The Illustrated American*, 1894. Under $6.

Page 60: Postcard, girl in red cape, The International Art Publishing Co., c.1907. $1-2; Trade card, girl and dog, no imprint, c.1890. $3-5; Postcard, children with gifts in doorway, Raphael Tuck & Sons, c.1914. $4-7; Postcard, children with apples, c.1910. $3-5; Postcard, girl in red at door, Raphael Tuck & Sons, c.1910. $2-3.

Page 61: Postcard, girl in red by M. Dulk, c.1912. $4-6; Postcard, angel with children, Germany, c.1907. $2-3; Postcard, child and green Santa, Germany, c.1906. $9-13; Postcard, blue-robed St. Nicholas at door, c.1905. $15-18.

Page 62: Postcard, children and pigs, Raphael Tuck & Sons, c.1907. $8-10; Postcard, cat in oval, 1907. $2-4; Advertisement for Christmas cards, 1893. Under $3; Postcard, angel leads horse, Germany, c.1907. $3-6.

Page 63: Untitled poem from Frank Leslie's *Popular Monthly*, 1893; Postcard, cats with violets, c.1910. $3-6; Postcard, girl in blue, c.1910. $1-2; Postcard, cats in silver lattice, c.1910. $4-7; Postcard, photo-type, children with umbrella, Saxony, c.1908. $2-4; Postcard, photo-type of children with roses, c.1912. $1-2; Postcard, boy with puppy, c.1907. $3-6; Postcard, puppy pulls cat in sleigh, Raphael Tuck & Sons, c.1912. $3-6.

Page 64: Lines from "Christmas Flowers" by Adelaide A. Procter, 1870; Trade card, girls give gifts to the poor, Manufacturer's Fire And Marine Insurance Co., c.1890. $12-15; Postcard, Santa with man and woman, "His Christmas Gift," by Charles Dana Gibson, c.1907. $15-20.

Page 65: Lines from "Christmas Around The World," by Margherita Arlina Hamm, 1896; Postcard, Santa with corncob pipe, Julius Bien & Co., 1908. $12-15; Postcard, Santa with feather pen, Julius Bien & Co., 1908. $12-15.

Page 66: Postcard, Santa by fireplace, c.1909. $8-12; Postcard, Santa in circle, c.1911. $8-10.

Page 67: Postcard, blue St. Nicholas, c.1907. $18-23; Die cut scrap, blue St. Nicholas, c.1890. $15-25; Postcard, red St. Nicholas with pack of toys and tree, c.1908. $12-15; Postcard, white St. Nicholas with red hat, Raphael Tuck & Sons, c.1909. $14-16; Trade card, white St. Nicholas gives apple to child, Jersey Coffee, c.1883. $15-20; Postcard, red St. Nicholas with deer at window, c.1913. $12-15.

Page 68: Illustration, "Old Father Christmas" from *Godey's Lady's Book*, 1867. Under $8; Postcard, girl hugs Father Christmas, H. I. Robbins Publishing, 1906. $14-18; Postcard, St. Nicholas puts candies in window, Germany c.1907. $12-15.

Page 69: Postcard, St. Nicholas holds wooden horse, c.1910. $14-18; Trade card, brown robed St. Nicholas, Joseph Horne & Co., 1889. $15-20; Postcard, St. Nicholas in white carries staff and tree, c.1908. $14-18. (This is sometimes found with a hold-to-light image of children in the snowy space, bringing the value to $40+)

Page 70: Illustration, "Merry Old Santa Claus" by Thomas Nast for *Harper's Weekly*, 1881, courtesy of the Dover Publications Archives Series. Under $15.

Page 71: Lines from an unsigned poem in *The Ladies' World*, 1901; Illustration and poem, "A Visit From St. Nicholas," by Clement C. Moore, from *Harper's Monthly*, 1857. Under $10.

Page 72: Lines from "December" by Frank Dempster in *St. Nicholas*, 1887; Postcard, Santa in loaded sleigh, c.1912. $8-10; Postcard, Santa makes sled, 1911. $12-16; Postcard, Santa with a polar bear, c.1909. $6-8; Postcard, Santa writes in book, c.1914. $12-15; Postcard, Santa holds doll, c.1913. $14-18; Postcard, Santa holds small tree, c.1910. $8-10; Illustration, "The Workshop of Santa Claus 1873," from *Godey's Lady's Book*. Under $10.

Page 73: Passage from "A Christmas Memory" by Albert Bigelow Paine in *The Philadelphia Inquirer Christmas Book*, 1899; Postcard, Santa looks over chimney, c.1916. $8-10; Postcard, Santa steps into chimney, c.1908. $8-10; Illustration, "The Christmas Station" by Thomas Nast for *Harper's Young People*, 1885. Under $15.

Page 74: Postcard, Santa hangs gifts on tree, Julius Bien & Co., 1908. $8-10; Postcard, Santa fills stocking, 1910. $3-5; Postcard, Santa holds doll, 1911. $12-16.

Page 75: Illustration, Santa and sleeping child by fireplace, from *St. Nicholas*, 1887. Under $10;

Page 76: Lines from "The Wail Of Santa Claus" in *The Philadelphia Inquirer Christmas Book*, 1899; Postcard, Santa at telephone, c.1907. $6-8; Postcard, Santa on locomotive, c.1910. $4-7; Postcard, Santa with flying machine, S. Bergman, 1917. $4-7; Postcard, Santa in auto, Henderson Lithographic Co., c.1918. $8-10.

Page 77: Quote from "Talks With Fathers And Mothers" by Margaret E. Sangster in *Good Housekeeping*, 1900; Postcard, photo-type, "Santa Claus's Letter Of Thanks," F. G. Henry & Co., 1910. $3-5; Postcard, Santa in white fur trim cap, Saxony, c.1912. $10-15; Postcard, Santa in black fur trimmed cap, S. Bergman Co., 1913. $8-10.

Pages 78-79: Lines from *Poor Robin's Almanac*, 17th century; Illustration, "Merry Christmas" by Kenny Meadows c.1853. Under $10; Postcard, jester tickles woman's nose, B. B. London, c.1914. $2-3; Postcard, woman in holly dress, Julius Bien & Co., c.1908. $6-10.

Page 80: Postcard, girl waves poinsettias beside sled, Stecher Litho. Co., c.1912. $1; Postcard, boy wears wreath, girl holds reins, Gottschalk, Dreyfuss & Davis, c.1913. $6-10; Postcard, December 25, c.1908. $1; Postcard, "Nimble Nicks" dance around tree, Whitney Made, c.1913. $10-15; Postcard, woman in bell, c.1908. $2-3; Postcard, woman in black by Archie Gunn, National Art Company, c.1908. $3-6; Postcard, woman's face in holly, c.1909. $3-4.

Page 81: Lines from "Christmas Carols" in *Frank Leslies' Chatterbox*, 1881; Postcard, angel in silver and purple lattice, c.1910. $3-4; Postcard, two angels in a circle and holly, c.1908. $2-4; Trade card, die cut scrap angel on brown board, Hamilton's House of Music, c.1886. Scarce, $15-20; Illustration, "The Christmas Party," from *Godey's Lady's Book*, 1867. Under $3.

Page 82: Postcard, choirboys, c.1910. $2-3; Photograph, church interior, c.1885. $4-6; Postcard, "O Morning Stars Together...," c.1912. $1; Postcard, girls in church, Whitney Made, c.1910. $3-5.

Page 83: Passage from "Talks With Fathers And Mothers," in *Good Housekeeping*, 1900; Illustration, "Singing Christmas Carols," *Peterson's Magazine*, 1879. Under $3; Greeting card, carolers, with poem, c.1873. $3-6; Postcard, caroling children, P. Sander, 1908. $2-4; Illustration and music, "Christmas Carol," from *Harper's Young People*, 1885. Under $3.

Page 84: Greeting card, boy and girl in nightdress read book, Hildesheimer & Faulkner, c.1883. Scarce, $15-18; Trade card, girl, doll, and cat, Woolson Spice Co., c.1885. $12-15.

Page 85: Passage from "A Christmas Memory" by Albert Bigelow Paine in *The Philadelphia Inquirer Christmas Book*, 1899; Trade card, child dreams of